TODAY'S TAP DANCING

by Rebecca Rissman

CAPSTONE PRESS
a capstone imprint

Snap Books is published by Capstone Press,
1710 Roe Crest Drive, North Mankato, Minnesota, 56003.
www.mycapstone.com

Library of Congress Cataloging-in-Publication Data is available
on the Library of Congress Website.
ISBN 978-1-5435-5443-4 (library binding) — 978-1-5435-5447-2 (eBook PDF)

Summary: Learn about the history and current trends of tap dancing and what it takes to be a
professional in the field today.

Editorial Credits
Gena Chester; editor; Kay Fraser, designer; Morgan Walters, media researcher;
Tori Abraham, production specialist

Photo Credits
Alamy:Pictorial Press, 21; Getty Images: FOX, 5, Hulton Archive, top 7, NBC, 15, Steve Mack, 29;
iStockphoto: AndreasKermann, Cover; Newscom: akg-images, 9, Barry Talesnick/ZUMAPRESS,
bottom 19, Glen Stubbe/ZUMA Press, bottom 13, JM11/Joseph Marzullo/WENN, 25; Shutterstock:
agsandrew, design element throughout, Elenadesign, bottom 17, EQRoy, top 13, Gingo Scott, bottom
11, Jack.Q, top 11, julkirio, design element throughout, KBYC photography, top right 27, Nicholas
Piccillo, top 17, Oleksandr Nagaiets, bottom right 23, ReVelStockArt, design element throughout,
Timonina, top 23, Ververidis Vasilis, top 19, Wunigard, bottom 7, ZenStockers, design element
throughout, Zvonimir Atletic, bottom 27

Printed in the United States of America.
PA49

Table of Contents

Syncopated Ladies. 4

Tap's Roots. 6

Becoming a Tap Dancer. 12

Going Pro in Tap. 18

Break a Leg!. 24

Glossary 30

Read More 31

Internet Sites 31

Index. 32

CHAPTER 1

Syncopated Ladies

A woman walks out onto a stage. She's wearing a black and white outfit. Her hair falls into her face as she looks down at her feet. Then the music starts. Beyoncé's voice rings out over the speakers. The woman's feet begin to rhythmically tap on the floor. More women join her from each side of the stage. Soon, they are jumping, spinning, and stomping. All the while, their feet tap a complex **rhythm** along with Beyoncé's song. When the song ends, the dancers stand up and smile. They are out of breath and sweaty. The audience cheers wildly. They loved the show!

The dancers are called Syncopated Ladies. They have been **viral** stars since 2012. And within months after Beyoncé shared a video of them tapping to her song "Formation," the music superstar invited the tap group to perform at the opening ceremony for the release of her clothing line, Ivy Park. Today, Syncopated Ladies are a female powerhouse tap group.

rhythm—a regular beat in music, poetry, or dance
viral—quickly and widely spread through social media

4

Syncopated Ladies performing on So You Think You Can Dance.

CHAPTER 2

Tap's Roots

Tap has roots in multiple cultures. It likely developed from dance competitions that were held in big cities in the mid to late 1800s. At these contests, dancers performed a variety of movements. Some did rhythmic moves that had their roots in African tribal dance. Others did Irish, Scottish, or English clog dancing. Clog dancing involved rhythmic movements done while wearing wooden-soled shoes, or clogs, that clacked on the ground. The dancers at competitions learned from one another. They adopted movements and rhythms that they liked.

By the 1920s, tap dancing evolved into what we know today. Dancers nailed or screwed small pieces of metal called taps onto the soles of their shoes. They used these taps to make noises on the ground while they danced. In 1921, dancers in a show called *Shuffle Along, or the Making of the Musical Sensation of 1921 and All That Followed* first wore taps on stage. Their style of dancing was called tap dancing.

At the beginning of the 20th century, tap dancers became a popular part of **vaudeville** shows. These traveling entertainment shows featured 10 to 15 acts, from comedians to singers to magicians.

vaudeville—stage entertainment made up of a variety of songs, dances, and comic acts

BILL "BOJANGLES" ROBINSON

Bill Robinson was born in 1878 in Richmond, Virginia. He spent much of his childhood dancing. By age 8, he began dancing in beer halls for money. At age 9, he joined a touring dance troupe. Robinson later went on to dance in vaudeville shows. He became known for dancing on the balls of his feet and a light, swinging style of tap dancing. In 1928, he performed in a show called *Blackbirds of 1928*. He famously performed on a set of stairs. He tapped rhythmically up and down the steps. This act made him very famous.

Robinson went on to perform on Broadway–the first African American to do so–and in many films. In 1935, he appeared in *The Little Colonel* with child star Shirley Temple. The two performed his stair dance together. This was the first time an interracial pair had danced onscreen together.

Traditional clogging—dancing with hard shoes that don't have metal taps attached to the bottom—still occurs today.

In the first half of the 20th century, tap dancing was a common skill among stage stars. But tap was popular among film stars too, and many movies featured it. Tap dancers developed their own unique dancing styles. This helped them stand out and make a name for themselves.

Gene Kelly was a famous actor and dancer during this time. His tap dancing was influenced by ballet. His performance of "Good Morning" in the 1952 film, *Singin' in the Rain*, showed his incredible skills. He leapt onto stairs, off of them, and across the floor with grace and style.

Tap began to fade from popularity in the late 1950s. It remained a relatively unpopular style of dance until Savion Glover and Gregory Hines emerged in the 1980s. Hines and Glover performed in the 1989 film *Tap*. Glover also performed in the 1995 Broadway show *Bring in 'da Noise, Bring in 'da Funk*. Their revolutionary style and skill helped revive tap and made it appealing to a new generation of dancers.

For his efforts in Singin' in the Rain, *Kelly (left) received an honorary Academy Award "in appreciation of his versatility as an actor, singer, director and dancer, and specifically for his brilliant achievements in the art of choreography on film."*

Fact

In the early 1930s, some of tap's most famous moves came out of a small African-American club in Harlem, New York, called the Hoofers Club. Today, many new tap moves and ideas come from yearly tap festivals, such as the Chicago's Rhythm World or New York City's festival, Tap City.

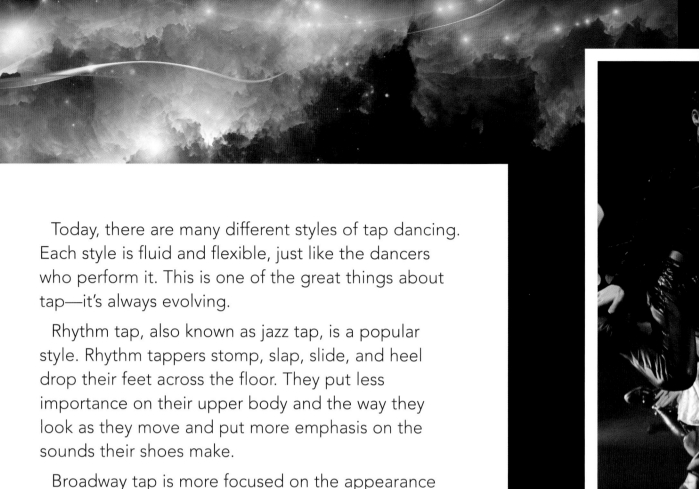

Today, there are many different styles of tap dancing. Each style is fluid and flexible, just like the dancers who perform it. This is one of the great things about tap—it's always evolving.

Rhythm tap, also known as jazz tap, is a popular style. Rhythm tappers stomp, slap, slide, and heel drop their feet across the floor. They put less importance on their upper body and the way they look as they move and put more emphasis on the sounds their shoes make.

Broadway tap is more focused on the appearance of the dancer's bodies than the sounds they make. Broadway tappers move their arms and legs in careful motions. Where rhythm tap is all about how the dance sounds, Broadway tap is all about how the dance looks.

There are many other styles of tap. Soft-shoe tap focuses on the sound of the shoe without taps attached. Buck and wing is a flashy form of tap dance that borrows from Irish and British clogging. Classical tap combines tap, ballet, jazz, and **acrobatics** to make its own unique style.

acrobatics— movements borrowed from gymnastics, such as handstands, flips, and forward rolls

a modern tap performance by the Hungarian dance troupe, Experidance

Some street performers use tap dancing to attract crowds.

CHAPTER 3

Becoming a Tap Dancer

Many dancers learn tap in a dance studio as young as two or three years old. Children in beginning tap classes learn basic steps. They learn to make noises with their taps, to jump, and to slide their feet. These early classes are fun and playful.

Advanced tap classes continue to focus on fun, rhythm, and creativity. Dancers learn to make additional sounds with their taps. They learn faster, more complex steps and rhythms. Many also study other types of dance, such as ballet and jazz. These help them to stay flexible, strong, and well-rounded.

Not all tap dancers follow this traditional path. Many people do not start dancing tap as children. They learn to tap in adult dance classes. Others do not take classes at all. Some learn to tap dance from online tutorials or books. These are great resources for people who are not able to attend classes in a dance studio.

Michael Wood did not learn t
until he was 18 years old. Even
he did not immediately becom
good dancer. It was not until he
junior in college that he finally
comfortable dancing. Wood di
his late start slow him down. He
passionate about dance. He wo
to become the best tap dancer

As an adult, he has achieved
successes. He has danced in the
Broadway musical, *Fela!*, toured
and Japan in *42nd Street*, and ap
in *Riverdance*.

42nd Street is the story of a small town girl who pursues her dreams of being a Broadway star.

Many people of all ages tap dance to stay physically and mentally healthy.

Regardless of where they learn, there are some movements that most dancers know. Some of these are very basic. A shuffle step, ball change, heel-step, and step-heel are all basic building blocks of a tap dance **routine**. These are simple movements that create noise on the ground. Dancers combine them in different ways to make powerful, rhythmic dances.

The Shim Sham is a sequence of movements that many tap dancers know. It dates back to the 1920s. Today, the Shim Sham is still an important part of tap. Recently, dancers began staging Shim Sham **flash mobs** around the world. Some of these large-scale performances took place in Canada, Germany, England, and the United States.

routine—a set pattern of movements in a dance
flash mob—a group of people that shows up at a specific time in a public area to perform a dance
choreographer—a person who arranges dance steps or action scenes

Fact
Many tap dancers use social media to reach new viewers. Chloe Arnold, who created Syncopated Ladies, has more than 70,000 followers on Instagram.

KYLE VAN NEWKIRK

Kyle Van Newkirk is a **choreographer**, dancer, and teacher from Nebraska. In 2015, he won the World Championship of Tap. In 2017, he competed on the first season of the television show, *World of Dance*.

Today, Van Newkirk travels the world teaching a unique style of tap that is influenced by hip-hop and contemporary dance. Van Newkirk encourages tap dancers to make tap fun and exciting, to think creatively, and to use their whole bodies when they dance. Props are also common in his routines.

Kyle Van Newkirk performing on World of Dance.

Tap dancing is great exercise for the whole body, not just the feet. Tap dancers develop strong muscles in their legs, core, and back from the repetitive movements of the basic tap steps.

Dancers must take good care of themselves in order to perform their best. That means warming up and stretching before they dance. This process usually takes between 10 and 20 minutes. After they dance, tappers stretch again for about 20 minutes.

Tap dancers must also get enough sleep and eat healthy meals. Tap can be a very demanding type of dance. Dancers can burn more than 300 **calories** in an hour of tap dancing. They must make up for this calorie loss with healthy, protein-rich meals. Without proper **nutrition** and care, dancers are at risk of injury. Uneven dance floors, slippery shoes, or a crowded studio can all lead to falls, slips, or crashes.

calorie—a measurement of the amount of energy that food gives you
nutrition—food that your body can use to help stay healthy and strong

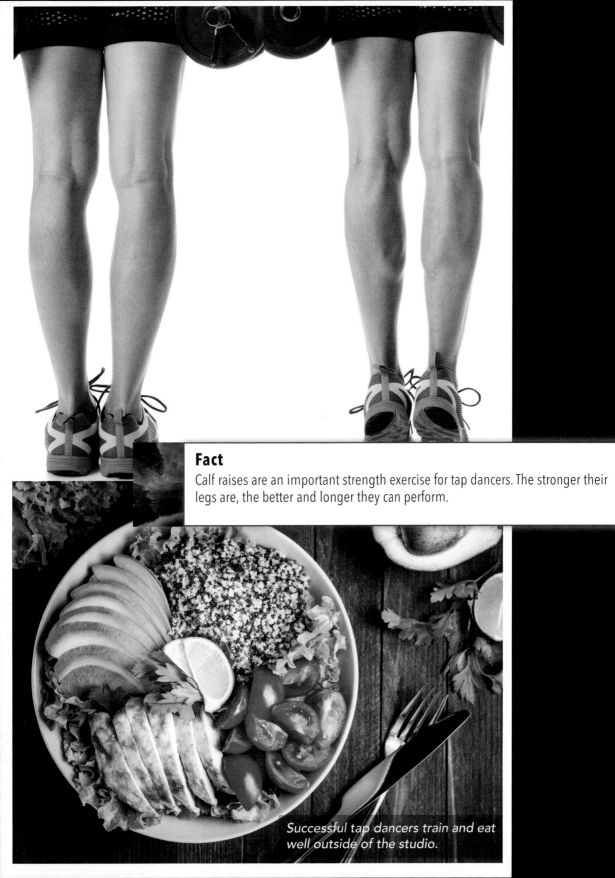

Fact

Calf raises are an important strength exercise for tap dancers. The stronger their legs are, the better and longer they can perform.

Successful tap dancers train and eat well outside of the studio.

CHAPTER 4

Going Pro in Tap

There are many types of stage performance careers for talented tap dancers. Some dancers pursue careers on Broadway. Some shows, like *Thoroughly Modern Millie*, *Anything Goes*, and *42nd Street*, have many tap dancing numbers. Other Broadway shows, such as *A Chorus Line*, feature tap among many other styles of dance. Most Broadway dancers need to be well versed in dance styles such as jazz, tap, ballet, modern, and even ballroom.

Broadway isn't the only place for professional tap dancers looking for stage work. Tap dancers can find careers in Cirque du Soleil, an entertainment company that produces circus-style shows around the world. Cirque dancers often combine tap with acrobatics and acting to give audiences an unforgettable show.

Finding a stage performance job in tap isn't easy. Dancers must make it through difficult **auditions**. These often last several rounds. Very few dancers who try out for these jobs are chosen.

audition—a tryout performance for a dancer

The first official tour of Cirque de Soleil happened in 1984. The troupe traveled through Quebec, Canada.

The musical Thoroughly Modern Millie *came to Broadway in 2002 but is set in 1922, a time when tap dance was very popular.*

Tap dancers who want to perform don't have to limit themselves to the stage. They can also find work in television, in movies, and even online.

Television shows such as *So You Think You Can Dance*, *World of Dance*, and *America's Got Talent* often showcase talented tap dancers. These shows help give their performers a wide audience. Then after the show, these dancers can use their fame to build up their careers. They can travel and perform on stage. Or they can visit local studios to teach or provide choreography.

Recent films have highlighted tap. In the 2016 hit film, *La La Land*, actors Emma Stone and Ryan Gosling sing and tap across the screen. In 2012, Jennifer Lawrence and Bradley Cooper tap dance in part of their final dance number in *Silver Linings Playbook*. These films have helped to remind viewers that tap dancing can be a current, exciting style of dance.

Some tap dancers perform for online audiences in tap tutorials, performances, and short clips. Doing this allows them to reach a wide audience. Pineapple Dance is a dance studio in London, England. It posts dance videos to its social media accounts. More than 45,000 people follow its Facebook page.

Emma Stone and Ryan Gosling in La La Land

Not all tap dancers look for performance careers. Some tap dancers become dance instructors. Others become choreographers who design moves for dancers to perform. In these careers, people can spend their days inside dance studios, listening to music, and dancing.

Other jobs for tap dance lovers take them behind the scenes. Tap dancers can use their expertise to become costume designers, lighting **technicians**, stage managers, **set** designers, and **videographers**. These jobs are all important to tap performances. Some tap dancers who enjoy writing can become dance writers or journalists who report on dance performances for blogs, magazines, and newspapers.

technician—a person who is trained or skilled in a technical area
set—the stage where a performance takes place
videographer—a person who records performances with a video camera

SEAN & LUKE

Sean Jones and Luke Pilalis are two tappers who appeared as a dance duo on *America's Got Talent* in 2014. They won over the judges by dancing to hip-hop songs such as Young MC's "Bust a Move" and Digital Underground's "The Humpty Dance." The tapping pair also charmed the audience with their friendship and obvious love of dance.

They used their television fame to find successful tap careers. Today, Pilalis is a dance teacher in Bloomington, Illinois. Jones continues to perform. He has been a cast member in *Hamilton*, the hit Broadway musical. He has also danced in *Jesus Christ Superstar, All Shook Up*, and *Jerome Robbins' Broadway*.

A lighting technician adjusting the lights before a performance.

CHAPTER 5

Break a Leg!

Tap dancing often looks carefree and spontaneous. Dancers joyfully tap out a beat to the music while leaping, sliding, and spinning around the stage. But most tap routines are carefully rehearsed. Lots of work goes into each performance.

Each routine starts with a choreographer. In tap, choreographers think carefully about how to use a dancer's tap rhythms to complement the lyrics and beat of a particular song. They also consider what, if any, props should be brought into the dance. Once choreographers have created their full dances, they break it into smaller segments and teach it to the dancers. These first lessons usually do not involve music. After the dancers have mastered the small sections of dance, the choreographer helps them link the whole song together. Finally, the dancers try the whole routine with music.

Tap dancers then rehearse, or practice, the song over and over. This helps them get familiar with the routine. It also helps them become confident with their movements.

Fact
Savion Glover specializes in rhythm tap, a style that uses all parts of the to make sounds.

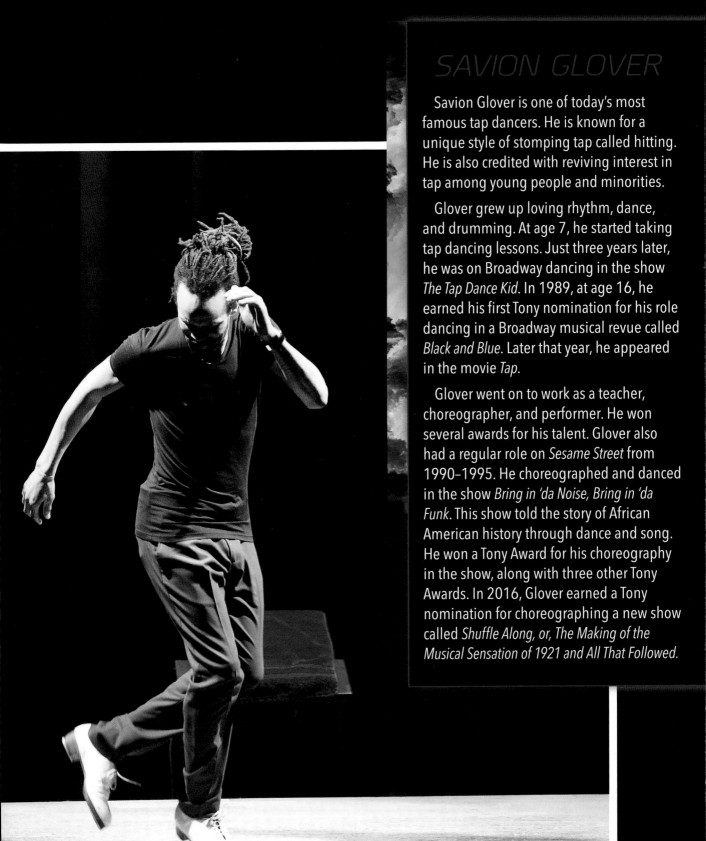

SAVION GLOVER

Savion Glover is one of today's most famous tap dancers. He is known for a unique style of stomping tap called hitting. He is also credited with reviving interest in tap among young people and minorities.

Glover grew up loving rhythm, dance, and drumming. At age 7, he started taking tap dancing lessons. Just three years later, he was on Broadway dancing in the show *The Tap Dance Kid*. In 1989, at age 16, he earned his first Tony nomination for his role dancing in a Broadway musical revue called *Black and Blue*. Later that year, he appeared in the movie *Tap*.

Glover went on to work as a teacher, choreographer, and performer. He won several awards for his talent. Glover also had a regular role on *Sesame Street* from 1990–1995. He choreographed and danced in the show *Bring in 'da Noise, Bring in 'da Funk*. This show told the story of African American history through dance and song. He won a Tony Award for his choreography in the show, along with three other Tony Awards. In 2016, Glover earned a Tony nomination for choreographing a new show called *Shuffle Along, or, The Making of the Musical Sensation of 1921 and All That Followed*.

All dancers usually do at least one dress rehearsal. This is a practice performance in full costume. Dress rehearsals usually take place at the performance location. This helps dancers get a feel for the lights, stage, and setup.

Dress rehearsals can be especially important for tap dancers. They need to feel and hear their taps on the stage. Understanding how the sound carries in the performance room can affect how they dance. They might stomp a little louder or try to make some movements quieter. Dancers who perform with live musicians use their dress rehearsals to make sure they can hear the music properly.

Many professional tap dancers alter their tap shoes to get the right sounds. Some screw the metal taps onto the soles of their shoes tightly. Others prefer their taps looser. Some even buy custom-made tap shoes. One popular trend is to glue or screw taps onto the soles of fashionable sneakers.

Dress rehearsals are done in full costume.

On the day of a big show, many tap dancers have a routine. This helps them feel ready to perform. Mara Davi, the star of *Dames at Sea*, has a tried-and-true pre-show ritual. Davi likes to start her day doing something relaxing. She spends time with family. She drinks plenty of water. Then, she takes an afternoon nap no later than 4:30 p.m. This helps her make sure she has plenty of energy for the show. She gets to the theater two hours before the show starts. There she spends about 30 minutes doing yoga in her dressing room. This helps her stretch and warm up her muscles. After that, it's hair, makeup, costume, shoes, and show time!

Broadway shows often last about two hours. This can mean a lot of **strenuous** dancing for the stars. Other types of tap performances are even more demanding. The Rockettes are a famous dance company that work in a variety of styles. During their performance season, they perform up to five 90-minute shows a day! Rockette dancers must be careful to stay healthy and take care of themselves to keep up with their schedule.

After a show ends, tap dancers go backstage. They take off their makeup and costumes. They put their tap shoes away. Then they head home. Many dancers soak their feet in ice after a show. This helps reduce swelling. They eat a late, healthy dinner. Finally, they go to bed. As they drift off to sleep, some dancers might think about the steps and rhythms they want to try next. After all, tap today is a fresh, exciting, and constantly evolving style of dance.

strenuous—difficult or challenging, especially on the body

Glossary

acrobatics (AK-ruh-bat-iks)—movements borrowed from gymnastics, such as handstands, flips, and forward rolls

audition (aw-DISH-uhn)—a tryout performance for a dancer

calorie (KA-luh-ree)—a measurement of the amount of energy that food gives you

choreographer (kor-ee-AH-gruh-fuhr)—a person who arranges dance steps or action scenes

flash mob (FLASH MOB)—a group of people that shows up at a specific time in a public area to perform a dance

rhythm (RITH-uhm)—a regular beat in music, poetry, or dance

routine (roo-TEEN)—a set pattern of movements in a dance

set (SET)—the stage where a performance takes place

strenuous (STREN-yoo-uhss)—difficult or challenging, especially on the body

technician (tek-NISH-uhn)—a person who is trained or skilled in a technical area

vaudeville (VAWD-vil)—stage entertainment made up of a variety of songs, dances, and comic acts

videographer (vid-ee-AHG-ruh-fur)—a person who records performances with a video camera

viral (VI-ruhl)—quickly and widely spread through social media

Read More

Hutchison, Patricia. *Women in Dance*. Women in the Arts. Minneapolis: Abdo, 2018.

Jones, Jen. *Top Dance Tips*. Top Sports Tips. North Mankato, Minn.: Capstone Press, 2017.

Lanier, Wendy Hinote. *Tap Dance*. Shall We Dance? Lake Elmo, Minn.: Focus Readers, 2018.

Internet Sites

Use Facthound to find Internet sites related to this book.

Visit www.facthound.com.

Just type in 9781543554434 and go!

Index

42nd Street, 13, 18

All That Followed, 25

America's Got Talent, 20, 22

Anything Goes, 18

ballet, 8, 10, 12, 18

Beyoncé, 4

Bring in 'Da Noise, Bring in 'Da Funk, 8, 25

careers, 18, 20, 22

Chorus Line, A, 18

Cirque du Soleil, 18

classes, 12

contemporary dance, 15

Dames at Sea, 28

Davi, Mara, 28

Fela!, 13

Hines, Gregory, 8

hip-hop, 15, 22

injuries, 16

jazz, 10, 12, 18

Kelly, Gene, 8

La La Land, 20

movements, 6, 14, 16, 24, 26

   Shim Sham, the, 14

meals, 16

Pineapple Dance, 20

props, 15, 24

rehearsals, 24, 26

rhythm, 4, 6, 7, 10, 12, 14, 24, 25, 28

Riverdance, 13

Robinson, Bill "Bojangles," 7

Rockettes, 28

routines, 24

Savion, Glover, 8, 25

Shuffle Along, or, The Making of the Musical Sensation of 1921 and All That Followed, 6, 25

Silver Linings Playbook, 20

Singin' in the Rain, 8

So You Think You Can Dance, 20

stretching, 16, 28

styles, 10

   clogging, 6, 10

Syncopated Ladies, 4

Tap, 8

taps, 6, 10, 12, 26

Thoroughly Modern Millie, 18

Van Newkirk, Kyle, 15

Wood, Michael, 13

World of Dance, 15, 20